**W9-AWP-440**

Children of
CUBA

THE WORLD'S CHILDREN

Children of
CUBA

written and photographed by

FRANK STAUB

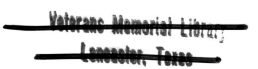
 Carolrhoda Books, Inc./Minneapolis

For all my Cuban friends and the dreams of their homeland; para todos mis amigos cubanos y los sueños de su patria. And for Jan—May her tropical island dream come true.

Carolrhoda Books, Inc. c/o The Lerner Group
241 First Avenue North, Minneapolis, MN 55401

LIBRARY OF CONGRESS CATALOGING-IN-PUBLICATION DATA

Staub, Frank J.
    Children of Cuba / written and photographed by Frank Staub.
        p. c.m. — (The world's children)
    Includes index.
        Summary: Presents the history and customs of Cuba while following a variety of children in their daily activities.
        ISBN 0-87614-989-1
        1. Cuba — Social life and customs — Juvenile literature. 2. Children — Cuba — Social life and customs — Juvenile literature. [1. Cuba — Social life and customs.] I. Title. II. Series: World's children (Minneapolis, Minn.)
    F1760.S73 1996
    972.91 — dc20   95-52673

Manufactured in the United States of America
1 2 3 4 5 6 – JR – 01 00 99 98 97 96

Imagine a land where thick flocks of parrots fly across the sky, and a thousand kinds of delicious fruit grow on the trees. A place where the air smells sweet, and the weather is always warm and moist. That's how Christopher Columbus described Cuba after his first visit there in 1492. Columbus called Cuba "the most beautiful land that human eyes had ever seen."

Cuba was one of Columbus's first stops after he sailed from Spain. He was hoping to travel to Asia to find gold and other valuable goods, and he thought Cuba was a peninsula sticking out from that great continent. First he sailed along Cuba's north coast. On a second voyage in 1494, he explored the south coast. He claimed the land as part of Spain. He also met some of the Taino people who lived there. Since Columbus thought he was near India, he called the native people Indians.

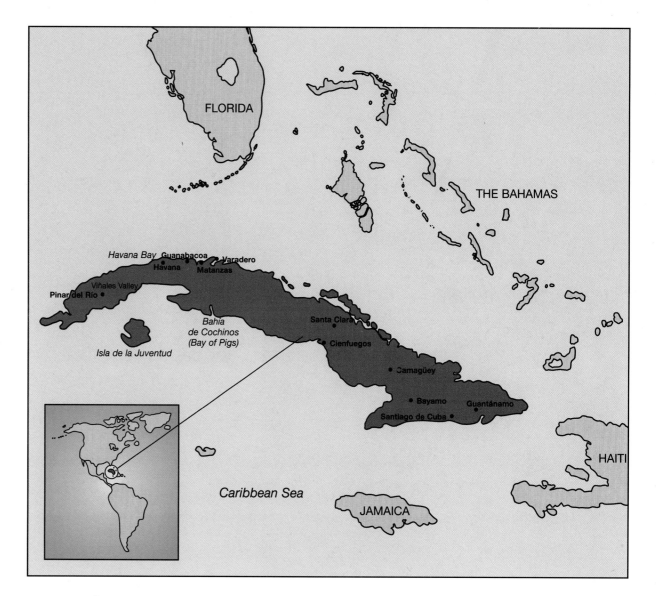

Raúl and Edel are both mestizos.

Chicon el Indio, one of the few modern Cubans who calls himself an Indian

After three months in Cuban waters, Columbus's crew grew homesick, and talked him into returning to Spain. But more Spanish explorers soon came to the island, looking for gold. During the early 1500s, they forced the Indians to work in the gold mines or on the Spaniards' farms. It was hard work, and the Indians were treated badly. Many died from overwork, and many others were tortured and executed. Great numbers of Indians were also killed by diseases that the Spanish carried to the island. Some even killed themselves because they were so unhappy. By the end of the 1500s, almost no Indians were left in Cuba.

Raúl and Edel have some Indian blood and some Spanish blood. Both speak Spanish, which is Cuba's official language. In Spanish, a person who has both Indian and European ancestors is called a *mestizo*. About one-fifth of Cuba's population are *mestizos*.

Top: *Spanish settlers built Morro Castle to guard Havana Bay in the late 1500s.* Bottom: *Children playing at another of Havana's old castles*

By the mid-1500s, most of Cuba's gold had run out. But there was still plenty of gold and other natural resources in other parts of the New World. A great bay on Cuba's northwest coast was the perfect place for gold ships traveling between Spain, Florida, Mexico, and South America to take on food and water. The bay was also a good place for ships to hide from pirates who wanted to steal the gold.

In 1515, the Spaniards had built a city next to the bay and called it Havana. Havana Bay was one reason Spain called Cuba its "key to the New World". Without Havana, it would have been much harder for Spain to conquer so much land in the Americas. The Spanish continued to control Cuba for most of the next 400 years.

Havana is now Cuba's capital and largest city, and the ocean is still important to its people. Much of Cuba's food, fuel, and other needs come in on ships. For Yosvany, Yardan, and Lizardo, the ocean is a great place to play. They're jumping in the water along Havana's rocky shoreline.

Right: *Yosvany and Lizardo watch Yardan jump into the sea.*
Below: *Cuba's former national capitol building is now a museum.*

Duanys lives in Santiago de Cuba, the country's second largest city. In school, Duanys is learning about the Cuban patriot José Martí. Martí wrote poems and essays and gave speeches. His words helped inspire the Cubans to fight Spain from 1895 to 1898, and win their independence.

Duanys is leaning on a cannon on San Juan Hill. The cannon is a memorial to Cuba's fight for independence. In 1898, a group of American horseman known as the Rough Riders helped the Cubans capture San Juan Hill from the Spaniards. The American fighters were led by Teddy Roosevelt, who later became the 26th president of the United States.

After Spain made peace with Cuba, in 1898, the United States governed Cuba for four years. Even after Cuba became fully independent, in 1902, the United States was Cuba's most important trading partner. Havana grew into a popular vacation spot for American tourists. Some Cubans worked with American businesspeople to start new businesses in Cuba. But most Cubans stayed poor, just as they had been under Spanish rule, especially in rural areas away from the cities.

Left: *Duanys leans on a memorial cannon at San Juan Hill.*
Above: *A statue of José Martí in Havana*

Above: *Children in the schoolyard at the old Moncada Barracks.* Below: *Bullet holes from Castro's attack still mark the barracks.*

Cuban leaders did little to help the poor. Fulgencio Batista, who came to power in 1933, was a harsh ruler who was hated by many Cubans. On July 26th, 1953, a young man named Fidel Castro led 110 brave men in an attack on the Moncada Barracks in Santiago de Cuba, where some of Batista's soldiers lived. The attackers lost the battle. But Castro steadily gained the support of the Cuban people. By 1959, he and his men had defeated Batista's army and taken over Cuba's government.

The Moncada Barracks have been turned into a school. Nelson is in the sixth grade there. His class is named for Roberto Rodriguez Fernandez, one of Castro's men who was killed in the battle for Moncada. Each class in the school is named for a different attacker who died.

A big '26' on top of the school stands for July 26th, the date of the Moncada battle. This date marks the beginning of the revolution that eventually freed Cuba from Batista. Today, parties, parades, and carnivals are held on July 26th, which is the country's most important national holiday.

Nelson (first row) and his sixth-grade classmates at the school in the old Moncada Barracks

The number 26 on top of the school marks the beginning date of Castro's revolution.

13

After defeating Batista, Castro became Cuba's president and set up a Communist economic system. Under pure Communism, the government owns all the business and is in charge of buying and selling everything. Communism's goal is equality and economic security for all. To try and reach that goal, Castro's government took over farms, oil wells, and other properties.

Some were owned by Americans. The leaders of the United States didn't approve of Cuba's taking over private property and becoming Communist. So Cuba turned to other Communist countries for support, especially the Soviet Union. The Soviets bought many of Cuba's products, gave it loans, and helped arm and train its army. All this meant the United States and Cuba were no longer on good terms.

After Castro's revolution, Cuban children studied Soviet history and Soviet heroes such as Vladimir Lenin. Yadil, Juan, Leosmani, Amer, Yoansi, and Roberto are playing in front of the first monument to Lenin in Latin America. Lenin was the father of Communism in the Soviet Union.

Yadil, Juan, Leosmani, Amer, Yoansi, and Roberto at the Lenin statue in Regla, near Havana

Right: *A monument to soldiers killed at the Bay of Pigs in 1961, when Cuban exiles, with the help of the United States, tried to invade Cuba. The exiles wanted to overthrow Castro's Communist government, but the invasion failed.*

Left: *A billboard in Santiago de Cuba celebrates the 35th anniversary of the Castro revolution. It reads, "Those who fight and resist, win."*

Roland's light-colored hair and skin suggest that his ancestors came from Europe.

Wherever their ancestors came from, most people living in Cuba were born there.

Even though Cuba once had close ties with both the United States and the Soviet Union, very few Americans or Soviets ever moved to Cuba permanently. The vast majority of Cubans were born in Cuba. Many are descended from the Spanish settlers who came to Cuba over the years. As a result, about one-third to one-half of all Cubans are white like Roland. But many Cubans who are officially listed as white have some African or Indian blood too. Through much of Cuba's history, there have been many marriages between people of different racial and ethnic backgrounds.

The story of Dunia's ancestors is just as sad as that of Cuba's Indians. After the Indians died off in the 1500s, the Spanish rulers kidnapped thousands of Africans from their homes and took them back to Cuba as slaves. First, the slaves worked in the gold mines. Later they worked on farms. But by 1886, all the slaves in Cuba had been set free.

Like Dunia's ancestors and those of about a third of all Cubans, most of Carlo's ancestors were African slaves. Some of the children he's playing with have ancestors who may have been slave owners. Cuba is a mixture of different ethnic groups, but nowadays that doesn't matter to most Cubans.

Right: *Dunia and her family are of African descent.*
Below: *Carlo (second from right) and his friends*

La Catedral de la Habana (Havana Cathedral)

Along with the Spanish language, the Spaniards brought the Roman Catholic religion to Cuba. Most Cubans are Roman Catholic, but many do not practice their religion. Catholicism is not as popular in Cuba as it is in Mexico, Puerto Rico, and other Latin American countries that were once ruled by Spain.

One of Cuba's largest churches is the great Havana Cathedral, built during the 1700s. Foreign visitors like to visit the cathedral. So Maria del Carmen sells the beaded necklaces she makes in a street nearby. Bargaining with the customers is part of her job. Maria del Carmen wants to get a fair price for her work.

There was a time when Cubans weren't allowed to sell things on their own because of the country's Communist economic system. But now the Cuban people may sell certain things without government help, just as people in capitalist countries like the United States can. Although Cuba is still Communist, it is not as strict as it once was.

Left: *Maria del Carmen bargains with customers.* Below: *This man makes his living shining shoes.*

Much of the food eaten in Cuba comes from other countries, and since the government doesn't always have enough money to buy foods from other lands, food shortages are common. The government allows Cubans to buy only a small amount of rice, beans, beef, bread, milk, potatoes, soap, toothpaste, and other basic items each month, but these foods can be bought at very low prices. Typical meals in Cuba consist of rice and beans, occasionally with meat. Many people who live along the coast try to catch fish to help feed their families. Josnel and Beni are hanging a hook and line into the water from an old dock in Havana. Recently, commercial fishing—selling the fish after catching them— has become an important Cuban industry.

Josnel (far left), Beni (in red shirt) and their friends fishing at Havana's waterfront

Left: *In Matanzas, Alberto tries to catch some tilapia fish to help feed his family.* Below: *The shelves of this grocery store in Campo Florido are nearly empty.*

21

Cuban shoppers wait patiently in line.

Cuba has few oil wells of its own, and the government can't afford to buy much oil from other countries. So gasoline is expensive. Even Cubans who can afford to own cars don't drive much because of high gas prices. Many people take the bus. But the buses keep breaking down, and there aren't always enough parts to fix them. Waiting for a bus can take hours. But Cubans are used to waiting. They form long lines when hamburgers, cooking oil, or other hard to find items are offered for sale, and hope there will be some left when they get to the front of the line.

With few buses, and with the high price of gas, bicycles are an important means of transportation in Cuba. The government gave Adoniz's father a bike to ride to work. But it was hard to pedal the long distance to his job. So he gave the bike to Adoniz and went back to taking the bus.

Above: *Adoniz (in back) and his friends.* Right: *A typical Havana street, with more bicycles than cars*

Adoniz's mother, Innocenta, works on a large vegetable farm. While she pulls weeds in the carrot field, another worker, named Pedro, waters the onions. Due to food shortages, Cuban people are growing more vegetables than they did in the past.

The farm Innocenta works on, like many large Cuban farms, is owned by the government. But Eliberio and most other small farmers own their own land. Eliberio's main crop is lettuce. He has no water pipe or hose reaching to his lettuce fields. So while his wife, Rosa, pours water from a sprinkling can, Eliberio walks back and forth to the well with a bucket.

Eliberio and Rosa's granddaughter Aliuska lives with them. Marisleidis, another granddaughter, lives across the road. The girls are proud of their grandfather, who fought with Castro against the dictator Batista and his army.

Top left: *Innocenta pulls weeds.* Above: *Pedro waters the onions.*

Above: *Eliberio and Rosa water a lettuce field.*
Right: *Eliberio, holding a picture of himself in his days as one of Castro's soldiers, with Marisleidis and Alluska.*

25

Although some of Cuba's farmers grow plants and vegetables or raise cattle, sugarcane is Cuba's biggest crop. Sugar and other products made from sugarcane have been Cuba's main export since the mid-1800s. Much of the world's sugar still comes from Cuba. Removing sugar from the sugarcane is one of Cuba's few major industries. But prices for sugar around the world are always changing, and Cuba often has trouble making the money it needs from sugar. In addition, the Soviet Union, which used to buy many of Cuba's exports, no longer exists, and the countries that made up the Soviet Union no longer support Cuba's Communist government. Depending so heavily on sugarcane has been bad for Cuba's economy and is one reason so many Cubans are poor. The government is trying to develop other industries and products so that Cuba won't have to depend so much on the sale of sugar.

Above: *Sugarcane growing on a plantation.* Right: *A view from above of some of Cuba's rich farmland*

Workers pull weeds at a Cuban farm. The government wants farmers to grow a variety of crops so the economy won't depend as much on sugarcane.

A tobacco farm in the Viñales Valley

Next to sugarcane, tobacco is Cuba's main crop. Alejandro and Jsmeli live with their parents on a tobacco farm in the Viñales Valley in western Cuba. Thanks to plenty of rain and great soil, Viñales Valley farmers produce some of the world's best tobacco.

Like most farm children, Alejandro and Jsmeli must do chores when they aren't playing or going to school. Jsmeli helps her mother cook and clean, and Alejandro works in the fields with his father. Besides tobacco, the family grows corn, beans, and grapefruit.

Alejandro and Jsmeli have finished their chores for the day, and their cousin Mileidis has come for a visit. The children are playing on the poles on which tobacco leaves are hung after they are picked. When the picking is done, the leaves are moved to a large barn for drying. After a month or so, the leaves are sent to Havana to be made into cigars.

Workers set freshly-picked tobacco on a rack. Later, the racks will be moved into a barn for drying.

Mileidis, Jsmeli, and Alejandro play on a tobacco rack.

Some farmland in Cuba is used to raise livestock, including sheep (left) and bulls (below).

Some of Cuba's land is used to raise cattle for meat and dairy products. Brahma bulls from India are mated with other kinds of cattle to produce animals that can survive Cuba's warm, humid climate.

In recent years, tourism has become an important part of Cuba's economy. Americans don't often visit Cuba, but visitors from Europe, Latin America, and elsewhere flock to Cuba's cities and beaches. With its beautiful hotels and beaches, the north coast town of Varadero is a tourist attraction for people from all over the world. Joan, who is visiting Varadero with his family, is making friends with a tame scarlet macaw named Pancho in a local park. Ana has a special friend too. Ana's mom works in a Varadero restaurant on the coast where a trained dolphin does tricks for the tourists. Ana has learned the hand signals that tell the dolphin to sing, shake hands, and kiss.

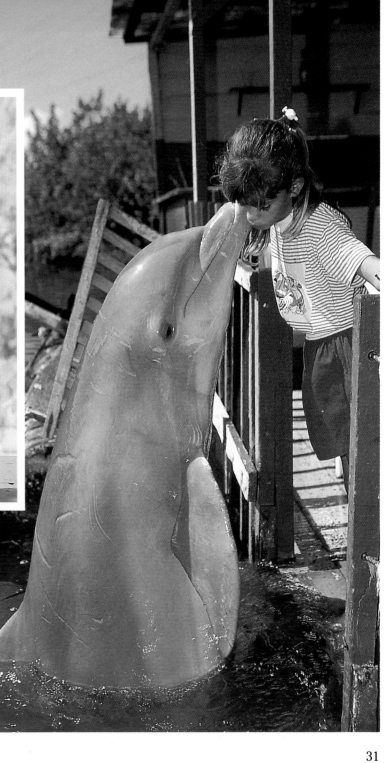

Ana (right) lives in the resort town of Varadero. Joan (above) is visiting from Havana.

Before they start school at age 6, many Cuban children go to day care centers run by the government. It's lunchtime at a day care center in the town of Campo Florido, near Havana. The children are having milk, yogurt, cheese, rice, bananas, bread, and eggs. Although food in Cuba is in short supply, day care and elementary students always get a free, nutritious lunch.

At another day care center not far away, Donaldo is playing doctor. Alejandro is the patient. The two boys may be very young, but they know what doctors do. That's because in Cuba anyone can see a doctor, even if they don't have any money.

In Batista's time, many Cubans didn't know how to read and write. So Castro set up government-run schools all over the country. All Cuban children are required to attend school until they are 12 years old. They are also encouraged to finish high school. Then if they want to, and have the ability, they can attend one of Cuba's many universities.

Opposite page: *Lunchtime at a day care center in Campo Florido.* Right: *At their day care center, Alejandro and Donaldo play doctor.* Above: *An elementary school classroom in Havana*

Daniel and Alejandro sweep the street as part of a special school work day in Santiago de Cuba.

Yudiguy is wearing her Pioneer uniform. The Pioneers is an organization for young people, like the Cub Scouts and Brownies. Pioneers meet after school and at summer camps. They learn crafts, play games, and learn various things about life and their country. Most Cuban children ages 7 to 11 belong to the Pioneers and wear their uniforms to school.

Cuban children are required to do some physical work as part of their education. Students at the Roberto Rodriguez Fernandez school in Santiago de Cuba are cleaning up the town. Daniel and Alejandro are sweeping the gutters. These work projects are meant to teach the students the value of physical labor. It also gives them a sense of pride in their city. On special work days such as this, the children don't wear their Pioneer uniforms.

Part of the school yard at the Catorce de Junio (June 14) Junior High School is a garden. Here the students learn how to grow plants for food and medicine. Today they are planting seeds given to the school by some American visitors.

Many Cuban high school students work for a company and learn a skill as part of their schooling. At the H. Uppman cigar factory in Havana, Chaster is learning how to make cigars. Chaster uses the best leaves as wrappers on the outside of each cigar and uses lesser-quality leaves as filler on the inside. Any tobacco that isn't good enough for cigars is sent to a cigarette factory.

Josiel, another student, is using a special press to make the cigars round and firm. Then he trims the cigars to the proper length, and another worker puts them in handmade boxes.

For a full year, Chaster and Josiel spend half of each school day at the cigar factory. After they graduate, they may work there full time. Most of the cigars they make are shipped to other countries. The boys take great pride in their work because Havana cigars are world famous for their fine flavor. Any kind of smoking can kill you. Yet business at the cigar factory is excellent.

Chaster (left) *and Josiel* (above) *at work at the Uppman cigar factory*

Alfredo, Miguel, and Barbara wear the uniform of their military school.

All Cuban men are required to serve 2 years in the military when they reach 18 years of age. Women can also serve in the armed forces. Alfredo, Barbara, and Miguel want to have their entire careers in the navy. To prepare, they are attending a military school.

Yesmin, Michel, and Raimys are studying electrical engineering at the Brothers Saiz University in the city of Pinar del Río. The Saiz brothers were two young men from Pinar del Río who were killed fighting for Castro during the revolution.

University students spend most of their time studying. After they spend 5 years at the university, the government will send them somewhere in Cuba to work. Yesmin, Michel, and Raimys don't mind being sent somewhere because that's how they can repay their country for giving them a college education.

Right: *Idolys, Yesmin, Michel, and Raimys take a break between classes at the Brothers Saiz University.* Below: *A monument to the Saiz brothers outside the university that bears their name*

Jorge and his teacher, Lazaro, with colored cakes honoring various Yoruba saints

Above: *Cooks preparing the food for the Yoruba party.*
Right: *Drum players and dancers at Jorge's party.*

In Guanabacoa, just outside Havana, there's a party for Jorge, who is training to become a Yoruba priest. The Yoruba religion, also called *Santería,* is a mixture of Catholicism and religions that slaves brought from Africa. Yoruba is very popular in Cuba, even among many people without African blood.

Becoming a Yoruba priest isn't always easy. Jorge must wear white for a full year. And he must learn much about Yoruba beliefs. But the road to priesthood can be fun too. Seven parties are held throughout the year in Jorge's honor, one for each of seven Yoruba gods or saints. Jorge's teacher is a well known Yoruba priest named Lazaro.

As the party goes late into the night, Jorge's friends and relatives dance to the beat of drums. Now and then a dancer touches his or her head to a drum so the music's spirit will enter their body. As more and more people touch the drums, the dancing gets wilder. Some people get so excited that they faint.

41

Much of Cuba's music and dance, such as the rumba, first came from Africa. The cha-cha and the mambo are also popular Cuban dances. Most Cubans love snappy rhythms. So a Cuban band may have more than one kind of drum, as well as rattles and other percussion instruments which are shaken, beaten, or scraped. Many Cubans also enjoy romantic ballads, especially the country's most-loved song, "Guantanamera." The words to this beautiful love song came from a poem by José Martí.

Leyma can hear beautiful music right in her own home. Her brother Cristo and their friend Eugenio are professional singers. Tonight they are practicing for an upcoming performance. Cristo has been singing since he was five.

Leyma wants to be a doctor when she grows up. But she's musical too. She takes lessons in piano and Spanish dance. Leyma and Cristo get much of their talent from their mom, Sylvia, who writes songs.

Above: *Cristo and Eugenio practice while Leyma works on her coloring book.* Right: *Leyma with her mother, Sylvia*

42

Above: *Cuban musicians perform at an outdoor restaurant in Havana.* Right: *Cristo and Eugenio sing "Guantanamera" for an audience.*

Basketball, dominoes, and soccer are all popular in Cuba.

Cubans like to play dominoes, soccer, and basketball. But baseball is Cuba's most popular game by far. Rene and Manuel play it every chance they get.

While Rene and Manuel play ball, a playoff game for the National Championship is just getting started between the provinces of Matanzas and Pinar del Río. Each province has one team in the Liga Nacional (National League), except Havana, which has two. When the United States and Cuba were on better terms, many players from the Liga Nacional went on to play in the American major leagues.

The New York Giants, Pittsburgh Pirates, and Brooklyn Dodgers all held spring training camps in Cuba at least once during the first half of the 20th century.

Pinar del Río won this game, by a score of 6 to 5. Rene and Manuel were disappointed. They were rooting for Matanzas, which is closer to their home in Havana. The boys sometimes wonder who would win a game between a Cuban National Championship team and the winner of the United States World Series. They hope some day such a game will happen.

Top left: *A national playoff game between Matanzas and Pinar del Río.* Above: *Manuel catches while Rene bats.*

MORE ABOUT CUBA

How big is Cuba?
The main island of Cuba is approximately 750 miles long. It is 124 miles at its widest point and 22 miles at its narrowest. More than 1600 smaller islands surround the main island.

How many people live in Cuba?
The population of Cuba is approximately 11 million. About a million Cubans live in the United States.

What are Cuba's main products?
Sugar, tobacco, nickel, coffee, seafood, and fruits are the main products Cuba exports to other countries.

What kind of weather does Cuba have?
Cuba's climate is semitropical, which means it is generally warm and humid. Rainfall is heavy from May to October.

What is Cuba's basic unit of money?
The basic unit of money in Cuba is the *peso.*

Pronunciation Guide

Catorce de Junio kah-TOR-say day HOO-nee-oh
Fidel Castro fee-DEL KAS-troh
Fulgencio Batista fool-HEN-see-oh bah-TEES-ta
Guanabacoa gwa-nah-bah-KOH-ah
Guantanamera gwan-tah-nah-MEHR-ah
José Martí ho-SAY mar-TEE
Liga Nacional LEE-gah nah-see-oh-NAL
Matanzas mah-TAN-sas
mestizo mes-TEE-so
Pinar del Río pee-NAR del REE-oh
Santería san-teh-REE-ah
Santiago de Cuba san-tee-AH-go day KOO-bah
Taino TY-noh
Varadero var-ah-DEH-roh
Viñales vee-NYAH-les

Index